8

PRINCIPLES FOR HUMAN-CENTERED LEADERSHIP

8

PRINCIPLES FOR HUMAN-CENTERED LEADERSHIP

THE YOUNG LEADER'S GUIDE TO CAREER HARMONY

JACK CHENG

INDIE BOOKS INTERNATIONAL

Academic All-America® is a registered trademark of College Sports Communicators

Book strategy by Leslie A. Rubin, www.imagematterzadvisors.com

ISBN-13: 978-1-957651-66-8
Library of Congress Control Number: 2024904090

Cover and interior designed by theBookDesigners
Art used on the cover by Lydia Cheng

INDIE BOOKS INTERNATIONAL®, INC.
2511 WOODLANDS WAY
OCEANSIDE, CA 92054
www.indiebooksintl.com

CONTENTS

FOREWORD

BY YOUNG LIU

*Chief Executive Officer and Chairman
of Hon Hai Technology Group (Foxconn)*

As a company leader in the ever-evolving landscape of the technology industry, I am deeply passionate about fostering technological innovation and nurturing the careers of industry talent. I've witnessed the transformative power of technology, and I believe that it holds the key to a brighter future for the next generation.

For those of you aspiring to enhance your career success in the dynamic world of technology, you'll discover a wealth of insights within the pages of this book. Authored by Jack Cheng, it is filled with eight principles that are not just inspiring but also invaluable. These principles can act as catalysts to propel your career to new heights.

It is not uncommon for many young individuals to feel uncertain about their career direction. Often, their focus gravitates more towards technology than interpersonal connections. However, Jack Cheng provides a solution to this challenge, and it's a solution that I wholeheartedly endorse.

Allow me to share the significance of Jack's role within the Hon Hai Technology Group (Foxconn). Today, I oversee the global operations of the world's largest electronics manufacturer and the foremost global science and technology solutions provider. In my capacity as Chairman, I set and orchestrate the company's strategic direction, propelling us into the next phase of international growth.

At Foxconn, our vision is to collaborate with leading customers worldwide to create a more interconnected world powered by smart technologies. We achieve this by delivering cutting-edge technology solutions to our customers and partners, and we are unwavering in our commitment to research and develop next-generation technologies in new industry sectors, products, and manufacturing processes.

Our primary growth strategy, known as the 3+3 strategy, encompasses three major industries—electric vehicles, digital health, and robotics—and three major technologies—artificial intelligence, semiconductors, and next-generation communication technologies.

Jack Cheng is instrumental in accelerating electric vehicle innovation and revitalizing American manufacturing through our resources and infrastructure in the United States via the MIH (Mobility in Harmony) Consortium.

I concur with Jack that we are living in an era of remarkable and rapid change. However, I also acknowledge the timeless principles that have guided my own career. These principles, such as the importance of loving what you do, fostering a growth mindset, giving back, and the five others detailed in this book, have withstood the test of time, and will continue to do so.

Education, of course, is essential. I look back fondly on my own educational journey, earning a Master of Science degree in Computer Engineering from the University of Southern California in 1986 and a Bachelor of Science degree in Electrophysics from Taiwan's National Chiao Tung University in 1978. But I can't stress enough that, to succeed in a career, you need more than a stellar education.

As Jack aptly emphasizes, these principles are interconnected. When all these principles harmonize, they create a positive flow and balance in your life, regardless of the world's ever-shifting landscape.

I wholeheartedly wish you a career filled with success and fulfillment.

Young Liu
TAIWAN

Jack Cheng and the MIH Project X Concept Car, the reference design for shared mobility.

Jack Cheng debuted the MIH Project X Concept Car at the Japan Mobility Show 2023.

Jack Cheng and the MIH team celebrated the unveiling of the Project X Concept Car at the Japan Mobility Show 2023.

PROLOGUE

Why Principled Leadership
Matters Now More Than Ever

The will to win, the desire to succeed, the urge to reach your full potential...these are the keys that will unlock the door to personal excellence. —CONFUCIUS, *ancient Chinese philosopher*

The beautiful thing about learning is nobody can take it away from you. —B. B. KING, *American blues guitar legend*

I attended the Japan Mobility Show in October of 2023, with my company MIH (Mobility in Harmony) Consortium, to unveil Project X, an open electric vehicle (EV) design platform. The launch of this smart mobility initiative highlights the central role EVs are playing in the development and success of smart cities—where transportation and other systems are effectively interconnected, coordinated, and managed.

We started Project X to provide partners interested in entering or expanding their role in the EV market with the freedom to create vehicles via a modular and highly customizable open system. This platform was developed to be not only open (with published standards so users and third-parties can edit it and build upon its uses) and agnostic (to operate equally well across various platforms), but also to create white-label products (which can be used and rebranded by companies) that can be tailored to the needs of any given market, from individual transportation to medical service vehicles to product delivery—every automotive use you can imagine.

As this book is being released, so is the Project X concept car, a three-seater small electric vehicle designed as the initial demonstration model. It is optimized for urban shared mobility such as ride sharing, rentals, and taxis. The launch of the Project X initial demonstration model is only the beginning, as corporations and communities connect to build various forms of sustainable transportation as part of a smart city master plan. Cars are much more than a means of getting from point A to point B.

I am always optimistic about the future. It is how I am wired. Yet, I understand people's concerns about how technology can shape our lives negatively. Everything I do in my work is focused on using technology to serve the needs of people and the planet. We need strong leadership to meet these challenges.

The openness, collaboration, and giving back exemplified by Project X reflect several of my eight primary principles for human-centered leadership developed over a lifetime. It is my desire to share these principles to benefit young leaders of today.

Why is this my focus right now? My resume tells part of the story: I served as vice president of Ford Motor Company in China for almost two decades. Since 2015, I have led NIO, XPT, and most recently MIH—all companies and initiatives focused on the present and future of EV and smart technology that is transforming not only how we drive but how we live.

The MIH Consortium is an open platform made up of thousands of members and dozens of working groups focused on every aspect of EV design and production. The aim is to establish designs and standards that bridge the gap for all members resulting in lower barriers to entry, accelerated innovation, and shorter development cycles.

I've lived in many places: Shanghai, Taipei, England, the United States, and Australia. It is wonderful to gain perspectives of people from so many cultures. Throughout my career,

I have had business relationships with people from all over the globe. I came to understand that, especially in business, we don't communicate across these silos of industry and geography the way we could, the way we should. For instance, at various times I was in a silo making cars for Europe, one making cars for the US, and one making cars for Australia. The silos didn't share information, so instead of creating a common platform to get things done and develop a more seamless experience for customers, we were all trying to do everything on our own. We all sold products, but what might have happened if we had worked together to solve challenges we had in common?

The vision of my current company, MIH, is to correct this tunnel vision. I want the next generation to see the value in building things together, to overcome barriers of language and culture in pursuit of common goals.

I have lived my life with a desire to find enjoyment and do what I can to make the world a better place. I know I have wisdom to share, but I know equally well that younger people have incredible insights to offer. Collective wisdom is a powerful resource. I am sharing these principles out of my own experience and the deep learning I have received from so many others along the way. It is my hope that younger people can combine this with the unique perspectives of youth to achieve great things as leaders.

My Need For Speed

I have spent my entire career around cars. I love cars. I appreciate the design, the aerodynamics, the mechanics, and the physics of how you can step into a vehicle and not only be transported from place to place, but also be transported emotionally by the experience. I've been on a lot of test drives in my life, and it is still a rush.

I remain in this business because that feeling has never changed for me. When I started at Ford Motor Company (more years ago than I care to count) I knew I wanted to be on a path of increasing responsibilities. I wanted to grow as a leader to be a benefit to the company and to live as full a life as I could.

The automotive industry is very different now. Cars are computers on wheels. What fuels cars is changing, too. The company I head today, MIH, is a leading voice in the industry when it comes to EV power. As electricity becomes the primary energy source for transportation and EVs become integral to the function of smart cities, MIH is always adapting; in every facet of life, we are all having to adapt to rapid change.

MIH's business model exemplifies this, beginning with our open EV platform, where we welcome all brands, developers, and auto supply-chain participants to become members of the Open EV Alliance.

Yes, I love cars, but throughout my career—from Ford, to EV maker NIO, and now with MIH—my focus has been about principled leadership grounded in building authentic, collaborative relationships.

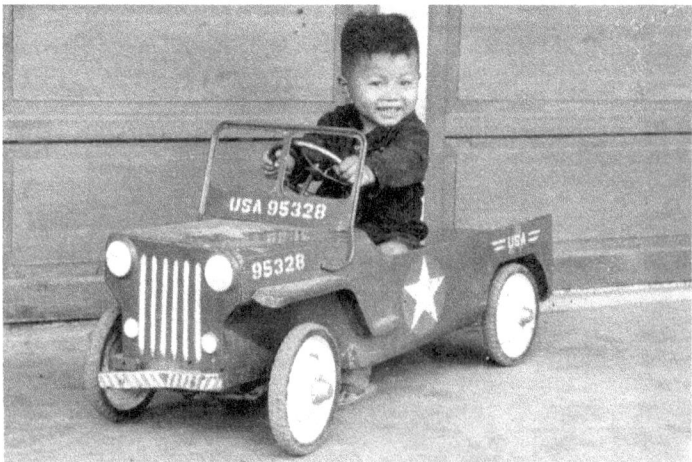

Little Jack beamed with joy in his toy car, a cherished gift from his father.

Calling All Young Leaders

So, while we are living in an era of incredibly rapid change, what does not change are the principles that have stood the test of time in my own career, and for the leaders who I admire in the world today. All these years in the industry and I'm still enthusiastic about what I do and what it means for the world we all live in. That enthusiasm stems from eight core principles.

These principles are:

Make human connections. Above all, be human. Be trustworthy, honest with yourself, and honest with others.

Love what you do. The only person who must love what you do is you. Not your parents, not your spouse, not your teachers, and not your friends. You be you and love what you do.

Always give back. Realize it or not, you've been given many opportunities that brought you to where you are today. Return that favor by giving back, whether others recognize it or not.

Have a growth mindset. If you set limits on your potential, that's as far as you will go. Take away those self-imposed limits and see where life takes you.

Go beyond yourself. Give 120 percent. Hustle provides great rewards.

Know your endgame. It's not just good to have goals, it's imperative. When you have a sense of what you are working toward, you know what to do next.

Build a community of allies. No one reaches their goals in isolation. A community of allies gets you there faster, and it's much more fun!

Adopt a philosophy of harmony. Life is all about balance and perspective. Keeping all the aspects of your world in harmony is a goal to keep reaching and recalibrating for.

You will see how these principles build on each other. Being your authentic self means being trustworthy and being able to trust others. Loving what you do makes it much easier to live that authentic humanity. It makes giving back, living without limits in a growth mindset, and giving 120 percent almost second nature. Being human also means being thoughtful and reflective about how you are living. What is your endgame, who are your "people" (your allies)? When all these principles are in harmony, there is an unmistakable flow and balance in your life, whatever the external circumstances.

Scott Miller wrote an article in *Inc.* magazine explaining the importance of aligning your values with your goals.[1] When you find your values and your company's values out of synch with your personal goals, you set yourself up for failure. You will only make yourself miserable. The earlier in your career you can align your values and goals, the more satisfied and at peace you will be.

Principled leadership is not just about short-term gains; it is about creating sustainable success. By making ethical decisions and considering long-term impacts, we can build a resilient organization that can weather challenges and adapt to a rapidly changing world. It's about fostering a culture that values integrity and holds us accountable for our actions. At the heart of principled leadership lies empathy, understanding, and the recognition that our decisions affect not only our employees but also our customers, communities, and the world at large.

Ultimately, principled leadership is a powerful force that can drive both individual and collective growth. I have seen this over and over in my career.

I'm at a stage in my life and career where I want to exemplify and amplify these principles with a new generation of leaders. One of the joys of my work and life is connecting with young people. I admire the young people I meet, and at the same time have concerns about the social isolation and human disconnection that can too often be features of life today. We are all still human and we are social creatures. Even in a digital world, we need to rediscover and commit to analog ways of making human connections. Finding this path is not always easy.

I want young leaders to know how to navigate these challenges in work and in life. The world is a big, beautiful place. I have been fortunate to experience so many different places, cultures, and people as I have worked all over the globe.

We are living and leading in remarkable times. I hope that by learning from the principles that have shaped my own leadership, you will find a path to a fun, fulfilling life in and outside of work.

1

PRINCIPLE 1
Make Human Connections

People will forget what you said, people will forget what you did, but people will never forget how you made them feel.

—MAYA ANGELOU, *American poet*

I've learned a huge amount because I've been tested and, more importantly, I've been trusted.

—PETE TOWNSHEND, *British guitar player for The Who*

You may think that the main job of a CEO is to concentrate on the bottom line and make decisions that keep the arrow of revenue pointing up. Obviously, paying attention to profits is important, but that is neither the starting point nor end goal of leadership.

I have been blessed with many good friendships over the years, with wonderful people inside and beyond the automotive industry. In this age when we can connect with anyone around the world, and yet loneliness is epidemic, it will not surprise you that building lasting friendships does not just happen on its own. I pay attention to that spark in a person that lets me know we have some things in common, enough to strike up a conversation over dinner or in the hallway after a meeting. When there is that commonality and camaraderie, a friendship can take shape. But that friendship needs to be tended over time. This, by some miracle of personality and persistence, has become second nature to me.

It may seem obvious that we all share a common humanity. But I have seen too often how a company's bottom line and shareholder value can take precedence over the people we work with and those who buy our products and services. That is a dangerous road, in my view.

That's why it is so important, now more than ever, to be uncompromising in promoting a human-centered approach to leadership.

Here is what I mean. To be truly human is to be in relationships with others. My relationships with my family members mean everything to me. Close friendships developed over shared interests—for me that would include cars and rock music—have also created deep connections and lasting memories.

We all spend a good deal of time at work, so human connection at work is essential. I appreciate the connections I make through work. I like to think I can count on close colleagues, and they can count on me, for challenges both inside and outside of work.

In every area of life, these relationship bonds are what make us human. They are the bedrock of a well-lived life. Human connection is vital to understanding ourselves and being open to the possibilities and potential all around us. Being human means building trust within those relationships. It is about building our own trustworthiness and growing in the trust of others. This sometimes requires radical honesty with us and with other people.

Living in the digital age means it is too easy to get disconnected from our humanity and the humanity of others. We can observe the world passively from a screen, or even divide our attention among multiple screens. A global pandemic showed us how much we could accomplish in this physically disconnected way of being, but it also exposed how important human connection is. So, we need human touch. We need the connection of face-to-face encounters to build strong relationships.

I've always enjoyed interacting with young people, and it's not just something I started doing as an elder. I've been doing it since I was young myself. I have a strong desire to see young people connect and create meaningful relationships.

I vividly remember a particular incident from when I first arrived in the US in 1985. When I landed in San Francisco, a former classmate from high school and college in Taiwan, who was attending UC Berkeley to study mechanical engineering, picked me up and took me to the campus. I then suggested that we have a party and enjoy the sunshine. My friend was always so focused on studying, and I thought he needed to take a break and have some fun.

We invited many of his classmates from UC Berkeley, and it turned out to be a fantastic party. The music was great. I was enjoying the evening, and I hoped my friends were too.

Reflecting on that experience, I realize that I had already started my formal career and had skipped pursuing a master's degree, instead moving to Detroit for work. I remember feeling that my peers who were still in school were jealous of me because I was driving the latest company car while they were still driving old, second-hand vehicles.

Meanwhile, I could appreciate the freedom they had as students without the responsibilities of full-time work. I wanted to impart some advice to my friend and his classmates, urging them to enjoy their time in school and not just focus on their studies. I encouraged them to have fun on campus, meet new people, dance with your partner like you are the only two in the world that evening, and understand what is happening in the world.

Through conversations with others, you can gain new perspectives and ideas. I reminded my friend and the other students that Albert Einstein eventually became a philosopher, not just an engineer or scientist, because he sought answers beyond what he learned in his field.

To truly grow and improve yourself, connecting with people and exploring the world beyond yourself is crucial.

Better Relationships Make You A Better Human

In an article in *Forbes* magazine, John Knotts writes about how companies can grow and stay human centered.[2] Knotts defines a human-centered company this way: "an organization that prioritizes the well-being and satisfaction of its employees, customers, and communities at large." He notes how businesses can do things like promote healthy communication and foster empathy. These concepts are not complicated and are fairly easy to navigate when a company is small. When a company grows, stakeholder concerns can cloud our view of how we can affect the broader community.

I believe that by connecting with others and broadening our horizons, we can become better versions of ourselves, and build better organizations.

If you are a workaholic, you won't know what your family is up to. What's the point? You're living to work, not working to live. Whenever someone comes to me with family issues that need to be taken care of, I think that should be their first priority.

Prioritizing family doesn't mean you're procrastinating or neglecting work. It's about looking at your life holistically and striving to do your best in every element. I think this spiritual aspect is crucial. If you don't have this spirituality, living in this world can be meaningless. Everything becomes work and living the life of a recluse.

A Human-Centered Relationship With Technology

At what point are technological advances a detriment to human civilization and the planet as a whole? This is a question we must always keep grappling with. That's why I believe so strongly that, as the EV universe continues to take shape and evolve, companies must remain human centered. That is a core value for us at MIH, and it is much more than just words in a corporate human relations handbook. We and our partners are developing ever more complex technologies, but these need to be first thought of as solutions to problems faced by humans and the planet.

My colleague Ted Lien wrote about this recently when he described the work of our testing and certification working group. He wrote, "Technological development is always faster than regulations. When new technologies are still developing, we have to conceive the content of testing and certification. When the working group puts forward the development

Jack Cheng in discussion with young talents at the MIH EV Design Award, embracing the fresh perspectives of the new generation.

results, there must be corresponding testing and certification projects to accelerate the implementation of the technology."[3] In other words, testing and certification must be in place to solve the problem and stay centered on the human factor in everything we do.

I often wonder how younger people think about the future. Based on my many interactions, I believe the future is in very good hands. While I still have a role to play, I want to do everything I can so the humans who come after me are in a better future than I can even imagine.

The MIH team unites, reflecting a shared vision and the collaborative spirit at the heart of innovation.

2

PRINCIPLE 2

Love What You Do

It had long since come to my attention that people of accomplishment rarely sat back and let things happen to them. They went out and happened to things.

—**LEONARDO DA VINCI,** *Italian polymath of the Renaissance*

To create something from nothing is one of the greatest feelings, and I would—I don't know, I wish it upon everybody. It's heaven.

—**PRINCE,** *American funk/R & B master*

Do you love what you do, or are you just earning a paycheck? This is a fundamental question we ask ourselves about work. When you are growing up, maybe you had dreams of becoming a famous artist, or a firefighter, or a key player on your favorite sports team. As we approach adulthood, our career expectations may change. But the desire to do something meaningful and fulfilling never goes away.

My love of cars led me to seek an engineering degree, which led to my first job out of college, with Ford Motor Company. Rising through the ranks at Ford, I never lost my love for the mechanics of how an engine runs or the aerodynamics of automobile design. After my many years at Ford, I could have become some kind of consultant or retired and worked on my golf game, but things were just getting interesting. The dawn of the electric vehicle was beginning. I had to find out what this new day would bring.

There is something I want to be very clear about. Loving cars and enjoying my work doesn't mean I don't enjoy life outside of work. For most people, I think finding work-life balance is a lifelong task. I have been very intentional over the years about maintaining this balance. I feel pretty good about my approach, but you'll have to ask my friends and family how I am doing!

After my tenure at Ford, I spent time working for the company that then owned Fiat. Among the many valuable lessons, I learned there: in Italian culture, decisions are rarely made in formal meetings. It is much more likely a decision will be made over dinner. *La bella vita*—a beautiful life—is cultivated in this way.

Fiat Chrysler CEO Sergio Marchionne asked me to join the company while he was overseeing the merger between Fiat and Chrysler. I learned that one hundred years ago or more, Fiat founder Giovanni Agnelli came to Detroit to visit the Ford production facility. He replicated this facility back home at Fiat in Torino. In a funny twist, since there was no room for a test track next to the facility, he built the test track on the factory roof. In a further twist of history, that building is now the luxury hotel NH Torino Lingotto Congress.

I learned some fun and fascinating things at Fiat, but those meals that stretched into hours—where business was done while life was lived—that is my major takeaway from my time there. I learned a way of living that reinforced my belief in the power of loving what you do as an expression of your zest for life—*la bella vita*!

Some people believe that loving what you do is a luxury that few can afford. We all need to earn a living, so their thinking goes to get a job that makes some serious money and find ways to have fun when you are off the clock.

That is a mindset that too many people have. While I don't think it is as simple as "love what you do and the money will follow," I do believe that a rewarding life—financial and otherwise—is much simpler when you are passionate about the work you do.

When I began my career, this was an easy equation for me. I love cars, so I got into the car industry. Now cars have become more and more computerized, but they are still cars. I don't have a deep passion for computers, but I have retained that passion for cars. So, I love what I do.

What has grown deeper is my love for what automobiles can accomplish as part of a wider system. When it comes to solving problems like traffic congestion in big cities, facilitating supply chains, ensuring people can quickly get to medical care during a health emergency—as well as simple things like getting your lunch order or the newest article of clothing or gadget for your home—smart, sustainable transportation is a part of all of these challenges. My work has evolved from "how can I make this car cooler and faster," to "how can I be a part of solving global challenges?" What is not to love about that?

In 2002, Jack stands with Ford's fourth-generation leader, Bill Ford, marking a century of automotive legacy.

MIH, Autoware, and TIER IV

Here is another prime example of why I love what I do. Autoware Foundation (AWF), TIER IV, and MIH are developing some amazing technology around autonomous-driving (AD) vehicles.

As consortium partners, together we developed an autonomous driving system using software design platforms from both AWF and MIH. Both these platforms are open, so that anyone can use them. Further, MIH and AWF worked together in order to ensure any platform can be used, so that a variety of companies can collaborate on autonomous driving projects.

Enter TIER IV, which is working on a major project in Japan, where the current market faces challenges in procuring affordable EVs certified for use for what is expected to be very high demand. In response, TIER IV has partnered with MIH and a number of other partners, developing custom design guidelines that provide basic information to advise car manufacturers on integrating AD features into EVs and testing them to comply with current standards.

Working together in an open, agnostic platform, TIER IV developed "fanfare," which allows customers to develop and operate AD-enabled EVs under their own brands. A minibus developed through fanfare is on the road as I write this, with many more projects in various pipelines.

Tier IV is working with MIH along with AWF to design these products standardized across geographical borders. With this system, third-party companies will be able to mass-produce models. With this kind of cooperation, the sky is the limit on what kind and how many EVs companies can bring to market.[4]

In the next generation of mobility, user centricity is the key. To enable developers to innovate and create great user experience and applications, we must work toward a future of software-defined vehicles—whose attributes and functions are mainly a result of software, not hardware—by realizing the Open EV Platform vision. This kind of sustainable mobility is why I remain enthusiastic about my work. I'm still loving what I do.

The Science Of Loving What You Do

Are you going to love your work every day? No. Sometimes your project does not get the green light from your boss. Sometimes you will be doing tasks that are not on your list of favorite things to do. You will have personality clashes with coworkers and bad days for what seems like no reason at all. So, loving what you do does not mean everything is perfect at work all the time.

But ideally, your work should align with your interests and talents. That's how I got into the car business, and even though computers are a tool that I have no great passion for, they serve a purpose. Cars still have four wheels and still make the journey potentially as fun as the destination. Whatever it is that interests you, that makes your heart lighter and your eyes brighter, you will not regret filling your days with that kind of energy.

In an article in *Fast Company*, Tomas Chamorro-Premuzic talks about the science behind job satisfaction and notes that for much of human history, work was work for most people, like it or not. You were born into a farm family, or your father was in a trade, like making bricks or blacksmithing. You went into that trade and made the best of it. We are fortunate to live in times when we have so much choice and opportunity available to us.

Chamorro-Premuzic goes on to suggest strategies like choosing well in the first place (that's what I did), along with the concept of "job crafting," that is, making the role your own by using your talents to boost productivity and play to your own strengths.[5]

Will you love every job you have equally? Probably not. But if you can find the right path, you will find the right fit with your role and the company you work for. If your path is the entrepreneurial one, you may find that loving what you do means striking out on your own. That is fantastic!

Counter-Programming Your Mind

Whether you work in an existing company, join a start-up, or build your own thing, there will always be obstacles to loving what you do. The voices saying you should just get work to pay the bills are powerful. Many will say, "Do what will make you money and then do what you love in your spare time. You'll be able to do that thing you love someday. Maybe you will find some weekends to pursue that, or, if not, when you retire." I see too many people hoping for time to do what they love in their spare time or "someday."

How do you foster the principle of doing what you love? It's not always easy. Growing up, my family did not have a lot. It would have been easy for me to chase a large paycheck and not worry if I enjoyed the work I was doing. But I always knew that wasn't the life I wanted for myself.

And it is definitely not the life I wanted for my children.

Both of my sons went to college in Michigan. That's when my Michigan friends Steve and Eva really became "Uncle Steve" and "Auntie Eva" to them. I met Eva as a colleague in the automotive industry, and my wife and I became dear friends with her and her husband Steve. I was so glad my sons had a support system nearby while in college.

My sons both graduated and went to work in the corporate world, just like their dear father. Of course, I was proud. But were they doing what they loved?

Here's how Auntie Eva remembers that time in their lives:

Jack's younger son, Huey, called me and said, "Auntie Eva, I wanna quit my job because it's not my passion." Huh.

I laughed and said, "Well, jobs these days are hard to come by. What do you want to do?" He said he wanted to open a restaurant.

I knew nothing about the restaurant business, and I knew no one in Jack's family had any experience with opening restaurants before. Huey had started working at a restaurant and really appreciated the chef, a very accomplished Japanese chef. This chef's dream was to open a restaurant like he had in Tokyo, but in New York City. Huey wanted to go to New York with this chef and start a restaurant.

The restaurant became very successful, and Huey not only had our support, but Jack really supported him as well. Huey had money set aside for graduate school, but Jack supported his decision to use that money for the restaurant.

My older son Jackson graduated and started working for a well-known consulting firm, the kind of job most people with an MBA dream of. You guessed it, he soon found out this wasn't his passion. He talked with me, and he checked in with Auntie Eva and Uncle Steve. Jackson also found his passion in the hospitality industry and now owns a successful bar and resort in Shanghai.

The funny thing about Eva's story is that I was able to return the favor soon. Eva and Steve's daughter wanted to study in Italy. I learned recently that Steve and Eva had observed how I was supportive of my sons, even though they were taking a path that was untested and far from risk free. Seeing how I had treated my sons helped Steve and Eva make the decision to help their daughter follow her dreams. She went to study in Italy—even though at the time COVID-19 restrictions meant her parents couldn't visit her. She even worked remotely for me as an intern for a summer.

Of course, we want our children to follow their passions, and ideally, they should see that modeled in our lives. Doing what you love is not selfish. It is fuel for you to live the life you want and to bring your best to your work and to your family.

I am in this business because of my love of cars. I don't particularly love computers and other technology, especially when they take away our interest in what is happening right in front of us. However, being able to work with my passion outweighs all that.

MIH is collaborating with global partners to target market growth in Japan, Thailand, India, the US, and more.

PRINCIPLE 3

Always Reach Out And Give Back

If you are kind, people may accuse you of selfish, ulterior motives.
Be kind anyway.

—**MOTHER THERESA,** *Albanian-Indian Catholic nun*

It is still a surprise when people tell me that I've had an influence
on them, particularly when it's someone I really respect.

—**BONNIE RAITT,** *American folk/country/blues icon*

In 1978, I was a junior at National Cheng Kung University in Taiwan. I won't say how often, but I was known to skip classes to spend time in the nearby port city of Kaohsiung. Don't do as I did—stay in school, kids!

One day, I overheard some US sailors talking about a Christmas party. The US Seventh Fleet was stationed in Kaohsiung. I was a singer in a band at that time. When I told them about my band they said, "You've got the gig." I brought my entire group to Kaohsiung to play. We had imagined it would be a small gathering of servicemen and servicewomen in a local bar, but this was no intimate get-together. They had rented out an entire hotel, and a few MPs were even outside making sure nothing got too out of hand.

This was at a time when the US military was withdrawing from Vietnam, and many service members were stationed in Subic Bay in the Philippines as well as in Kaohsiung. There were a lot of service people there ready for some R and R. That's what they were doing and why they were throwing a party. I don't remember what songs we played, but I remember being glad we could share our talents with this crowd. We were all enjoying ourselves.

I experience so much joy in giving like this. Anyone who knows me knows about my love of music. Sharing music at that time, against the backdrop of the conflict in Vietnam, is a vivid memory for me. I was glad to give back and share my love of music in this way.

Be willing to give of yourself, to give back with gratitude. This is a principle in Buddhism. Give first without expecting anything in return. Trust that you will receive back whatever it is you need in the moment.

For me, beyond playing music for strangers, this means building lasting friendships. I appreciate the people I have met over my life, and a few of these have become lifelong companions. We are there for each other. If relationships are based on what you can get out of them—a transactional approach—your life will not be as rich and fulfilling as it could be. I try to give without expecting anything in return. The beauty and magic of this approach to life is that in giving in this way, it is returned to you in wellbeing and knowing that your friends have your back the same way you have theirs.

Steve and Eva have been friends of the family for years. I had initially met Eva at a work meeting, and when we both worked for Ford in China, our families became inseparable. My wife and I visit them when we are in town, and they visit us. Eva's story in the previous chapter of being a listening ear to my children is an excellent example of reaching out and giving back—we have always done that for each other.

I also try to give back through mentorship. Right now, at MIH we have an internship program where young people learn about the power of collaboration in the EV ecosystem and beyond. I know it is a cliché to say it, but I learn at least as much from the interns as they learn from me.

Recently I found out that a current intern, Sean, came to MIH with the preconceived impression of me as a very serious person. He used terms like "authoritative" and "noble" to describe me, which is at once very kind and also makes me laugh a little bit. Sean's education is in marketing and so he joined that team at MIH. That is how I got to know him, and he got to know me.

When Sean was struggling with a big life decision, I was so pleased that he thought to reach out to me to discuss it. We had a meal together, and Sean shared his concerns. "Which path should I take?" is a question we all ask at various points in life. While I certainly did not want to tell him what to do, I could offer a perspective that comes with age and experience. It means so much to me to be a source of support and encouragement like this.

The Art And Science Of Giving

In his book, *The Most Good You Can Do*, author Peter Singer writes, "Effective altruists don't see a lot of point in feeling guilty. They prefer to focus on the good they are doing. Some of them are content to know they are doing something to make the world a better place. Many of them challenge themselves, to do a little better this year than last year."[6] Singer's research shows that the group he calls effective altruists are largely millennials. That is why I try to always keep learning from those younger than myself. I am inspired that this demographic cohort has such a firm grasp on the concept of altruism. On the other hand, leave it to a long-term businessperson like me to seek the most efficient ways of reaching out and giving back!

LESLIE RUBIN ON JACK CHENG'S PHILOSOPHY

I was contacted by Yen Chong, who is Jack's close friend, advisor, and god-father to his sons, in December of 2016. At the time, Yen was acting as lead recruiter and human relations person for Jack, who at the time was CEO of XPT Global and cofounder of NIO. They were looking for a head of communications for XPT. Jack liked my background of deep corporate communications and public relations, along with my leadership skills in running executive communications for C-suite leaders.

I started working for Jack in early 2017. Our first meeting was in a hotel bar in San Jose where he described his vision of the future for electric vehicles and how both XPT and NIO would fulfill this vision. Jack built a very special team, and I loved working with Jack and the marketing team out of Shanghai. While I spent most of my time looking for public relations opportunities, writing bylines, and getting Jack ready for speaking opportunities, I worked closely with the marketing team to develop the brand behind XPT.

I traveled to Shanghai many times to spend time with the team—be it Jack's first book launch or the Shanghai Auto Show—and I was always included as a key member of the team.

Jack has always surrounded himself with young and smart people. I honestly think that's what keeps him young at heart. Also, he has always associated with people who were well connected and motivated to get things done.

His philosophy has never swayed—creating a world for the next generation, one that is better than we have today. This was long before his sons had children and he became a grandpa. Jack's wife and sons are very important to him. He's been married to Lydia for *years*—she's lovely. And Jackson and Huey have become successes because of their father's encouragement and entrepreneurial spirit.

Give Back But Leave Some In The Tank

I'm an EV guy now but forgive a traditional fuel–based automotive metaphor. Giving back can be truly life affirming and a benefit to both the giver and receiver. On the other hand, it is important not to give to the point that you are depriving yourself of your own needs. You need to leave something in the tank for yourself.

Another valuable metaphor as we consider the principle of giving back is the airplane oxygen mask: make sure your own mask is secure before helping others secure their oxygen. You can't reach out and give back if you have no air. Put in automotive terms, running out of fuel, from an electric fuel cell or another source, is not good for anyone. So, make sure you have enough in reserves, emotionally and financially, so giving back does not deplete your own resources.

I sometimes wonder if the idea of self-care is more integrated into the Eastern worldview. From a Western perspective, recharging your own batteries is too often seen as a weakness. To this end, I came across an excellent article in the *Harvard Business Review* from contributor and leadership development coach Palena Neale. In the article, Neale asks two questions of her C-suite clients who are reluctant to talk about such things:

- If instead of focusing on "self-care," I invited you to focus on diet, sleep, exercise, and emotional regulation, how would you feel differently?

- What could you stop, start, or continue doing right now to improve your mental and physical health?[7]

Hopefully, younger leaders, wherever you are from, whatever your background might be, you can balance the desire to "never stop never stopping" in the hustle culture by paying attention to your own physical and emotional needs. Hustling can lead to fading too quickly, but knowing your own needs and responding to them will bring longevity to your career, and you will accomplish more in the long run.

Give Back Anyway

I've always liked that quote from Mother Theresa at the beginning of this chapter. Be kind, no matter what other people think about your motives.

But whatever people may think about your motivation, there is a greater cost in making every interaction transactional, trying to get more than you give as if life is some kind of monetary balance sheet. I am glad to help friends and give beyond that in quiet ways. If you try to keep the score "even" by paying attention to who is helping you and how much, you are missing the point. Generosity should be freely given, without expectation of return. The truth is, generosity breeds generosity, and you will find that you are receiving more than you give. I have no idea how that math works, but I have experienced this phenomenon over and over.

So, don't keep score of your good deeds. Just do them. Giving back as an act of gratitude and thankfulness is what life is all about.

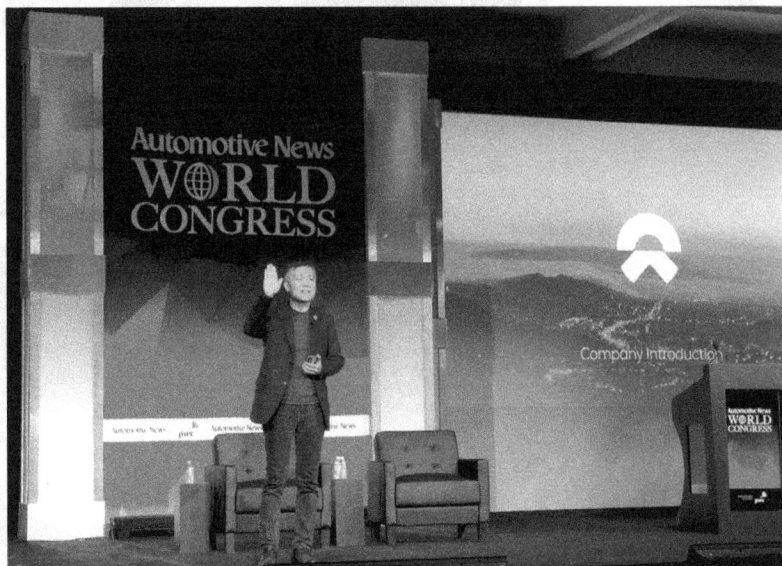

Jack Cheng, then co-founder of NIO Inc., addressed the Automotive News World Congress with expertise and vision.

Celebrating literary creativity, Jack Cheng at the release party of his debut Mandarin book, Jack, Just the Way You Are.

PRINCIPLE 4
Have A Growth Mindset

The past is a steppingstone, not a millstone.

—**ROBERT PLANT**, *English musician, guitarist for Led Zeppelin*

You don't have to be great to start, but you have to start to be great.

—**ZIG ZIGLAR**, *American author*

There is no one right path to reaching your goals. My own path to the role of CEO of an EV company took many twists and turns, right from the beginning.

For instance, I was never the student with the highest grades. Could I become an engineer and work in the auto industry? I thought I might need a graduate degree in order to even get in the door. But my grades were not going to get me into grad school at my preferred school, the University of Michigan. That would not be the path to my dreams.

And yet, I moved to Detroit. I knew I wanted to start my career in Detroit for two reasons: it was a major hub for the auto industry, and I loved the music of Motown.

I studied thermodynamics and got a mechanical engineering degree in Taiwan. Moving to the United States, to Detroit, I got a job with Ford, and I did get the opportunity to hear a lot of that Motown sound: Diana Ross, Stevie Wonder, and so much of the essential rock and funk music coming out of the city in those days. It was an education in itself. By day I was working on chassis engineering and brake suspension, and by night was enjoying the music of that era of the late 1970s and early '80s. What a time to be alive!

I could have let the prospect of not studying at the University of Michigan derail my plans. But I knew I could do the work and prove it in the Motor City. Later, Ford sent me back to China to work, and I kept moving up the ladder, even while I was playing gigs with my band every chance I got. I was finding my path.

Looking at the world with a sense of potential is the heart of a growth mindset. A growth mindset starts with a positive outlook. We want relationships to grow and business to grow. A positive outlook is needed to make all of this happen.

Any MBA professor or business leader will tell you that a growth mindset is essential. But what does that look like in a world filled with complex realities? What does a growth mindset mean in a world with finite natural resources? This is the kind of challenge I love to face. Growth does not have to mean "use up." A growth mindset is about embracing the potential and finding ways, against all odds, to tap into that potential.

You're Not "All Set"

I don't like the phrase, "I'm all set." It sounds like settling for less, like there is no ambition for more. Yet, this is a well-worn way of thinking. It is good to be content, but I believe there is a difference between contentment and a desire for even better things to come and the will to make that happen.

After a long career at Ford, I spent several years at Fiat. Then, when I was looking at what my next chapter would entail, I was looking at the bigger picture of the automotive industry.

The world was definitely moving from fossil fuels to renewable energy resources. That's when I got the germ of the idea that would become NIO, an EV company that starts with a car and looks way beyond to what EV can do to help shape the future. My friends Steve and Eva have been mentioned in previous chapters. They are both great sounding boards for whatever comes from my wild imagination. Here is how Eva recalls that time:

> *I remember when we were living in Dearborn, Jack would be in town for business frequently. As he was starting the car company NIO, most of us in the industry with the big three here thought, "You are trying to do the impossible." Not the idea of EV itself, but because Jack was going to put a car out on the road in three years. The standard here at the time to market from concept was four, five, even seven years.*
>
> *But because of his enthusiasm and confidence in what he was trying to accomplish, he was able to assemble and rally his team around working together to make this vision come to life. So, I was always really impressed by that.*

I don't mind taking on big goals when I know I can marshal people behind the idea. When we are all going beyond ourselves, there is not much we cannot accomplish.

The Brain Science Behind The Growth Mindset

I'm no neuroscientist, but here are some basics as I understand them. When we learn something new or face challenges, our brain forms new connections among neurons. These connections are like pathways that information travels along. The more we practice and learn, the stronger these connections become.

In a fixed mindset, people tend to stick to what they already know and are good at because it feels comfortable and safe. In a fixed mindset, when you encounter challenges or setbacks, your brain might interpret it as a sign of your limitations. To protect your ego, you revert to what is comfortable.

With a growth mindset, you are more prepared to embrace challenges and view failures as opportunities to learn and improve. It's important for me to remind myself that the brain is like a muscle that can grow stronger with exercise. That's how I keep pushing myself to learn and develop new skills, knowing that with effort and persistence, I can achieve more.

In an article from *Fast Company*, author Chris Hunter writes about how a fixed mindset is more binary: "This is possible" or "This is impossible."[8] Catching yourself when you start with these false either-ors can help you build a growth mindset. That's because the key to developing a growth mindset is to be aware of our thoughts and beliefs about our abilities. Whenever you catch yourself thinking, "I'm just not good at this" or "I'll never be able to do that," try to challenge those thoughts. Instead, remind yourself that with practice and dedication, you can improve.

Overcoming Stumbling Blocks To A Growth Mindset

You should not get the impression that a growth mindset is automatic or easy for me or anyone else. Even though I am by nature a positive person, a growth mindset is not always easy to maintain. Global economics do not care how positive I am. Trying and experimenting involves a lot of failure before success is borne out of all of that experimentation.

Following are a few lessons I have learned about maintaining a growth mindset even while facing adversity.

Acknowledge The Challenge

Buddhism has played a significant role in shaping Chinese culture. For a growth mindset, it provides a good starting point. Its concepts will be very familiar to some of you, but for those not already versed in these beliefs, the starting point of Buddhism is to acknowledge that suffering exists.

A growth mindset does not mean I ignore problems or potential problems. Buddhism also teaches about the path beyond suffering. This, to me, is the heart of a growth mindset. Challenging times are finite. How do you build beyond the challenges? That is where real growth can occur.

This is why I can look at technology not as a danger, but as a tool to enhance human life and better life in all forms. Yes, there is a climate crisis, but there are solutions within reach. A growth mindset puts my focus on the solutions beyond the problems.

You will always encounter stumbling blocks. This is a natural part of life. Moments of self-doubt are not a permanent state of affairs.

Use Challenge As A Learning Opportunity

Don't roll your eyes at this basic truth. Stumbling blocks provide us with invaluable opportunities for learning and growth. They force us to reevaluate our strategies, innovate, and become more resilient. Embracing these challenges can ultimately lead to greater success.

Adapt And Iterate

A growth mindset is not static. You are always learning. When one way doesn't work, you can quickly adapt and find another path. Iteration is just a process of trying something, working out the bugs, and refining them until you get the best results possible.

It took me a number of years to stop beating myself up

when a project did not go according to plan, or expectations were not met for any number of reasons. Learning from these experiences, rather than giving up or repeating them, is key to a growth mindset.

You Can't Reinvent An Industry Without A Growth Mindset

NIO is an EV automotive company that began out of this growth mindset. When I started NIO, we wanted to create a brand that began with an automobile but did not stop there. The NIO vision came to encompass not just vehicles but also power infrastructure and even homes. It was exciting to be a part of this, and I thought I would remain at NIO for the rest of my career. Then I got a call about a company that expanded exponentially on the vision of NIO.

With MIH, Foxconn Chairman Young Liu saw something that few others could see. The automotive industry up to this point had been a very closed system. To develop an open platform to build tools and products together could have been a nonstarter. To some, it was like trying to reinvent the wheel. Their thinking was that we already had systems in place and this effort would not flourish.

But that is not how growth happens. When I was asked to join MIH, I knew I could build on what we learned at NIO and expand the universe of players in this ecosystem. This kind of work, finding new ways to grow and flourish, is always exciting to me. And we are just getting started.

Jack Cheng stood proudly at the NIO Innovations exhibit, showcasing the company's advancements in EV chassis and body-in-white design.

Jack Cheng with winners and judges at 2023 MIH EV Design Award, bridging MIH with the bright minds of tomorrow.

PRINCIPLE 5

Go Beyond Yourself

There's still time to change the road you're on.

—JIMMY PAGE AND ROBERT PLANT,

English musicians from Led Zeppelin

Closely related to the growth mindset is the attitude that keeps you moving toward growth. You can't get where you want to go without putting in the effort. Pick your discipline—whether it is science, engineering, music, sports, art; those who go beyond themselves, beyond 100 percent, are the ones who achieve greatness.

That's what going beyond yourself means to me: giving 120 percent effort to reach your goals. And when you work with a team where all are inspired to go beyond themselves, that is when the magic happens.

I was in England once and went to a football match with my dear friend Roger. Manchester United was the home team. I don't remember who they were playing. Their stadium has four boxes, one for guests and the remaining three for home. However, there are many police officers in between because they are afraid of fighting. Basically, watching football is not about watching the game but about not getting into fights. My friend Roger and I had to shout just to hear each other.

Manchester United was Roger's team. The old fox got us seats in a VIP box. In the VIP box, there was a long-haired guy and his girlfriend. I asked my colleague, "Who is this guy?" He replied, "Oh, Jack, that's my friend, Robert Plant."

So, we were sitting near *that* Robert Plant at this football game—very cool. We spoke briefly and I asked if he would sign an album if I brought it to him at a future match. Later, when I went back to Taiwan, I bought his most famous album, known as *Led Zeppelin IV*, which had many great songs, including "Black Dog," "Rock and Roll," and "Stairway to Heaven." I brought back the CD to England to have him sign it the next time Roger and I were at a Manchester United match. Sure enough, there he was in those same seats in the VIP section. When he signed it, he asked me, "Jack, do you know if this is a knockoff? Many people sell fake CDs for money." I shrugged and told him I truly didn't know, and he still signed the album. It is a prized possession to this day.

Robert Plant is a great example of giving 120 percent, not just in going out of his way to interact with a fan, but through his whole career. Led Zeppelin was known in their early days for the mayhem they caused touring all over the world, but they are also well-known for their work ethic. Robert was a big part of keeping the band on task and building on their success.

He could have hung up his guitar after Led Zeppelin, but he continues to make music, tour, and surprise and delight fans along the way. I suppose I could have switched directions or slowed down after my years at Ford. I'm not comparing myself to Robert Plant (even though I do have some skills on the guitar!) but I knew I wasn't done after Ford. As I saw the advent of electric vehicles, the Internet of Things, machine learning, and other technological movements, I wanted to keep going beyond myself. I wanted to explore and be a part of moving forward collaboratively with EV and smart technology. I wanted to keep testing the limits of my mind and my leadership capabilities.

This principle goes hand-in-hand with a growth mindset. If you are "all set" you are not going to go beyond yourself. Trying your best is not good enough. You have to stretch yourself and then see if you can exceed the target. Go beyond expectation and push to the next level.

When I speak with younger people, I like to stress that you can't wait until you are "ready." You are ready to make an impact now. And while staying focused is good, I try to encourage people to not be too task oriented. I love the sense of accomplishment after a task is completed, but I try to remember that the work is never done. We are never "all set."

Intrinsic Drive

In his excellent book, *Drive*, author Daniel Pink describes the work of University of Wisconsin professor Harry F. Harlow, who, while running experiments with rhesus monkeys in which they were tasked with solving puzzles, discovered that the incentive to complete the task itself was a motivation beyond things like external punishment and reward—similar to the threat of losing your job or receiving a financial performance bonus. As Pink describes it, "the monkeys solved the puzzles because they found it gratifying to solve the puzzles."[9]

Fascinating. I totally understand this. Of course, earning a good living at a job and feeling secure is important, essential even. But going beyond and giving 120 percent is about more than that. When you feel gratified by the work you are doing and are accomplishing things as an individual and together with your team, it is so gratifying. Working in a good organization means you are making an impact greater than you could on your own.

Going Beyond For Customer Experience

Every company says they want to excel at customer experience. But how do you deliver on that? In the automotive world, design happens most often in the controlled environment of the engineering department. At NIO, I wanted us to go beyond the data we were gathering and the testing we were doing in-house.

For instance, when I was at NIO, I took a group of researchers and engineers to a nearby highway overpass. So, there was this big group of people in white lab coats looking down at the traffic. It must have been quite a sight. But I wanted them to observe the behavior of the drivers and passengers as they were just going about their commutes. One of the things we discovered is that women, when they were in the front passenger seat, would often put their feet up on the dashboard.

That is their business I guess, but it can be dangerous and also smudge up the windshield and dashboard. Was there a solution to this? What if we integrated a lounging position and footrest right into the design? We did just that, giving front passengers all the leg room they could possibly want. This became an incredibly popular feature.

When you think outside the R and D labs and boardroom, you find creative solutions. Care about user experience in this way, and you are going beyond and giving 120 percent.

There are young people all over the world raising issues around climate change and offering potential solutions. I spoke at Stanford University a few years ago, and I brought along two electric SUVs from NIO to highlight the power of EVs in creating a greener future. I love these interactions and learning from young people studying at places like Shanghai Jiao Tong University, Tongji University, and Youngstown State University. I encourage students every chance I get to explore their potential and make a meaningful impact as young individuals, rather than merely passing time until graduation.

MIH Testing And Certification
Working Group Goes Beyond

MIH is made up of a number of working groups. For instance, we have several working groups focused on safety and cyber-security. Working groups are a great method of keeping teams focused on particular projects and solving specific problems. The goal of the MIH testing and certification working group is to formulate testing and certification standards and assist other working groups. For example, one of the main subjects of discussion in the powertrain working group is the two-speed gearbox. This technology is now mainly used in cutting-edge sports cars. But what testing and certification are required when this technology is applied to electric vehicles? That's what the testing and certification working group wanted to know.

Technological development is always faster than regulations. As developers, we want to know what works and what does not; regulations can catch up with our high standards. However, when new technologies are still developing, we have to foresee the potential requirements of testing and certification.

The automotive industry has always attached great importance to testing and certification. It takes a long time for vehicle manufacturers to certify suppliers for compliance. If vehicle brands were to use unreliable parts, they would face the risk of automobile recalls. That's not in anyone's interest. In any industry, but especially one in which the product is out in public traveling at a high rate of speed, testing and certification must be taken very seriously to avoid both accidents and huge financial losses.

Entering the era of electric vehicles, the emphasis on safety has not changed. And previously existing standards remain, but also become more complicated, especially in the following three areas:

Motor, electric control, and battery. The working group looks at aspects of this area such as charging stations and charging piles. For example, in the past, gasoline vehicle batteries were 36V, which was enough to start the engine, but now the basic charging system of electric vehicles is 400V, and the latest trend is to upgrade to 800V. Changes in the battery system will also affect the management of infrastructure and power plant operations. These are all related to the regulations of each market. Governments will need to catch up and formulate new regulations so the EV ecosystem can evolve.

Safety. There are many safety regulations in the automotive industry, such as the well-known vehicle crash test regulations. There are many unknowns as we enter an era of technologies like autonomous driving and assisted driving. Different considerations are required, which makes testing more complicated.

Software. More and more software will inevitably originate not just standard from the manufacturer but imported into the car from third parties. This makes it necessary to deal with possible loopholes in the software.

In addition, different countries have different regulations. The testing and certification working group addresses these regulations. Since many members of the MIH Consortium are not from the automotive industry, the working group helps members master relevant testing and certification information and helps them understand what kind of regulations need to be complied with for different models and different markets.

The goal of the MIH Consortium is to lower the barriers to entry into the automotive industry through the establishment of standards. Therefore, the testing and certification working group has several tasks.

First, it must define the basic requirements of the quality control system in regard to vehicle regulations and assist MIH members in building relevant capabilities.

Second, the working group needs to help MIH members master the design, development, and inspection capabilities of the automotive industry. For example, the quality control process of the computer industry is different from the requirements of automotive original equipment manufacturers. In terms of software, the computer industry is familiar with software maturity management. However, the automotive industry has different quality control methods for software suppliers.

Third, the working group defines the quality inspection list so that MIH members can quickly examine their supply chains.

Fourth, MIH's testing and certification working group standardizes safety levels, safety requirements, and testing and certification standards, and assists member companies to develop products that can be successfully adopted by automotive customers.

Going beyond means staying ahead of regulatory bodies and making sure you are doing the absolute right thing for your customers and your business partners.

What Going Beyond Yourself Means And Does Not Mean

Going beyond yourself does not mean saying yes to every invitation and opportunity that comes your way. You have to be strategic about your own priorities and how they align with the company's priorities. When considering a move to a new position, whether it is a promotion or a lateral move within or beyond your current department, assess your interest, strengths, and willingness to learn new skills in this new role.

If it is the right move, great. But also, be willing to say no if it is not the right move.

Going beyond yourself is also not only about grinding out work. Work should not be a grind. When I started MIH, I thought, "we need a company song!" I had a friend from way back, John Hsuan, who is a very big deal in the semiconductor industry. Like me, he also loves music, and I thought he might want to write the lyrics. I said, "John, MIH needs a song. Can you give us some lyrics?" He sent over an excellent but very serious set of lyrics. I looked at them and thought, who wants a somber company song? I needed to take a different path.

One of our interns, Stephanie, had a background in music (that stuck with me from her resume). I had another friend write the music, and then asked Stephanie and her colleague Emily to write the lyrics. They came back from my friend's music studio in Hsinchu and shared with everyone who would listen what fun it had been. Stephanie's friends from college recorded the song, now with light-hearted lyrics, and it turned out beautifully.

Developing the MIH song is a wonderful example of living in harmony. When your life is in harmony and balance, going beyond yourself becomes a joy and not a challenge. It is bringing all of yourself to the work you do. When you accomplish that, there is such a feeling of alignment. You are where you are supposed to be and doing what you are supposed to do.

Building The Habits For Going Beyond Yourself

In his book *Atomic Habits*, James Clear begins by recounting the story of a traumatic injury he sustained as a baseball player in his second year of high school.[10] He was in a coma for a period of time, and then there was a long road to recovery. He was able to play baseball again, but he was benched for most of the rest of his high school career.

Maintaining his unique tradition, Jack brought his NIO colleagues to-gether to form a band, harmonizing the rhythm of teamwork with music.

By building habits around physical therapy and practice for the game, he was able to join the team at his college, Denison University, in Ohio. Eventually, he was a starter on the pitching squad, became captain of his team, and was named to the *ESPN The Magazine* Academic All-America team in his senior year.

Clear developed habits that helped him not only in the field, but to achieve academically and in many other areas of his life. No one would have blamed Clear if he had quit baseball after that horrible accident. But he did not let a setback side-track him.

One of the habits I keep up regularly is to practice and jam on my guitar. I literally take a guitar everywhere I go. Building that discipline into my routine may seem like a small thing. But, like Clear, small habits repeated over time can create an impact well beyond that one small, repeated act itself.

PRINCIPLE 6
Know Your Endgame

A journey of a thousand miles begins with a single step.

—LAO TZU, *ancient Chinese philosopher*

I think everybody has their own way of looking at their lives as some kind of pilgrimage. Some people will see their role as a pilgrim in terms of setting up a fine family or establishing a business inheritance. Everyone's got their own definition. Mine, I suppose, is to know myself.

—ERIC CLAPTON, *British guitar virtuoso*

What does it mean to know your endgame?

In part, this is about Simon Sinek's famous "knowing your why."[11] Know why you are getting out of bed each morning and doing the things you are doing. It is easy to go on autopilot and then you become David Byrne of the Talking Heads asking, "Well, how did I get here?"[12]

Knowing your endgame means taking the time to set not just business goals, but personal goals. It means making a plan and naming the benchmarks that will let you know you are on your way to achieving those goals.

Bill Russo has been my friend for a number of years. Having lived in the US and other countries throughout my career, I try to keep an eye out for foreign businesspeople and other expats living in my part of the world. Twenty years ago, that was Bill. He has since become a dear friend.

Here is how Bill recently described our friendship, and how it relates to our ultimate purpose and goals in life.

It is a cliché to say "it's a small world" when encountering a familiar person unexpectedly. For those of us working in the auto industry, it's an even smaller world, as paths often cross for people in this industry along their career journey. For those of us fortunate enough to have experienced the rise of China's auto market over the past few decades, we live in an even smaller world as we have shared this journey together.

I came to China in 2004 as the VP responsible for Chrysler's Northeast Asia business. The organization was then a part of DaimlerChrysler. After leaving Chrysler in 2008, I decided to remain in the small world of China's auto industry as it offered the most rewarding path for adventurous people with a passion for the industry. In that way, Jack Cheng and I have shared a journey.

During my time at Chrysler China, Jack Cheng was a VP of component design engineering, product planning, and product development at Ford China. I first came to know Jack after he became Chairman of China for the restructured Fiat Chrysler Automobiles (FCA). Jack, along with several other friends including Alysha Webb (formerly with Automotive News China*), and Ray Bierzynski (formerly with General Motors and later Chery Auto), were part of a club of China auto industry experts often referred to as the "Shanghai Mafia." We were sharing a journey in the "small world" of China's auto industry.*

Jack's journey is amazing, having led the Magnetti Marelli and FCA's businesses in China, after which he cofounded NIO—one of China's pioneering smart electric vehicle makers. Jack was the chief architect of the company's XPT unit, which was the group responsible for the underlying technology platforms of the company.

A few years ago, Jack told me he would be taking a new position within Foxconn responsible for expanding the company's role in the emerging electric vehicle industry. Given Jack's unique blend of experience with vehicle and technology integration, I felt that there was no person better prepared for the role of building the Mobility in Harmony (MIH) platform.

The automotive industry is being transformed by waves of technology innovation that has been accelerated in China, and I'm proud to see a member of the Shanghai Mafia emerge as the architect of this new global platform.

Without a planet for our children and grandchildren to live on, the game is over. That is why my focus for the past decade-plus has been on sustainability within and beyond the auto industry. Every time a new electric vehicle is developed, that is a win. By building an open EV ecosystem to experiment, collaborate, and build new ways of doing things, MIH is very much in the mix of taking on the biggest challenges of our time.

Building a sustainable future for people and the planet is my endgame. I think it is important to let go of notions that big dreams and big goals are too grandiose. I'm not saying everyone's endgame should be to change the world. But these principles build on themselves. Go after your endgame, whatever it is, with everything you've got. Don't limit your thinking. Be honest with yourself and others. When thinking about your endgame, that is the time to pull out all the stops.

How Do You Define Your Endgame?

Your endgame is not a static destination; it's a guiding idea that constantly inspires us to push the boundaries, innovate, and evolve. It's about embracing a growth mindset, continuously learning and refining your goals.

If you are early in your career, it might not seem important to think about your endgame. The opposite is true. You have to know where you are going and the ultimate goal so you can measure progress. At the end of the day, have I made progress toward my goals? You have to have the endgame clearly in mind in order to work toward it.

Goals should not only be far off, but for now. Live your life in rich and rewarding ways while you are working toward the endgame.

That's the value of life. Otherwise, why are you doing all this work for if not to enjoy a better life? A lot of people now, particularly the new generation, live to work. They're workaholics; when they go home, they don't even have a hobby. They don't enjoy music or painting or art. When you get old, you find that when you are by yourself, you are better off playing some music or creating some art. These are the things that make your life richer.

Don't put your career above everything. You should put your lifestyle above your career. That makes a huge difference, because if you put work and career ahead of lifestyle this can lead to unhappiness. A diverse life enhances your career and your happiness. This leads to a happier life when your career is done too.

The average lifespan for a Ford Motor Company executive after retirement who does nothing is five years. No, thanks. I wasn't going to take that path. I found new opportunities to make an impact. Don't lose your inertia.

I'm not suggesting that a good endgame is all work and no play. I've tried to emphasize throughout this book the importance of enjoying life at every stage.

For too many people, the uncertainty of the future is a license to just take life as it comes without planning or forethought. There is a lot to be said for "being present" and living in the moment. But there is a balance to be made between focusing on relationships in the present and planning for the future.

For me, having an endgame in mind and staying mindful of my goals helps me to enjoy the present that much more. I know where I am going, I know what is important to me, and that gives me a lot of freedom in the here and now.

The Endgame Is Not All About You

The endgame is not always about your far off, ultimate end-of-career goal. It's good to have personal goals, but what is the endgame for your organization? For us at MIH, the endgame is creating a user experience in EV that transcends the automobile. It starts with how an individual user interacts with a particular car. But it is also about creating a viable and long-lasting EV charging infrastructure. Ultimately it is about how society benefits from the potential of EV in the smart city and beyond.

August 8 is Father's Day here in Taiwan. Always August 8, not a certain Sunday of a certain month. So, it often falls on a workday. Another difference from American Father's Day: rather than an opportunity to receive gifts from their children, it is a time for fathers to express their appreciation and love for their children.

I did that with my children this past year, but it was a workday, so I spent a lot of the day with my work family. I gathered the team who were in the office and pulled out my guitar and we sang a few songs as a celebration for all the fathers in the room. What a great time.

My endgame is to be the best leader and the best father I can possibly be. I want to leave this world having done everything I can to make it more livable, and to make our living more sustainable. I want my team and my family to enjoy their lives and keep moving forward toward a better world.

Flexibility Is Crucial

Having an endgame does not mean knowing the future. I did not know where my vocational life would take me after my time at Ford. My endgame was more about the impact I knew I wanted to make, the kind of unfinished business—in a very broad sense—that I knew I wanted to complete.

This led me to decisions and opportunities. First with Ford, Fiat, NIO, and XPT, and now with what feels like a culmination at MIH. But still, I do not presume to know what the future holds. An endgame is more about an openness to possibility than a roadmap that one refuses to deviate from.

The MIH team and Jack celebrated their collaborative success at the MIH Demo Day 2022, marking a milestone in the open and agnostic EV revolution.

At MIH Demo Day 2022, Jack and his old friend filled the air with music, creating a harmonious backdrop for a day of innovation.

7

PRINCIPLE 7
Build A Community Of Allies

The fact is that relationships are the alchemy of life. They turn the dross of dailiness into gold. They make human community real. They provide what we need and wait in turn for us to give back.

— **JOAN CHITTISTER** *in* The Gift of Years

I've discovered that Motown and Broadway have a lot in common—a family of wonderfully talented, passionate, hardworking young people, fiercely competitive but also full of love and appreciation for the work, for each other, and for the people in the audience.

— **BERRY GORDY,** *founder of Motown Records*

I get by with a little help from my friends. This is one of my favorite Beatles songs, and an excellent principle to live by.[13] While I understand the importance of personal courage, perseverance, and tenacity—very important character traits one needs to build as a business leader—these personal attributes never operate in a vacuum. A climber on Mount Everest is making their own personal journey, but they are safest when they are traveling in a group and will likely not make it at all without seasoned guides to help them along the way.

Collaboration is essential in life and business. We cannot build something great in business in isolation. This is not something that can be faked. You cannot build a community of allies with a transactional mindset. I am talking about really being there for people, and believing they will have your back too.

Of course, in business, there will be times to build transactional alliances to meet a common goal, but that is not what building a community of allies is about.

During my time with NIO, I often held orientation events for new employees, at both the junior and senior level. I am always interested in the kinds of music people enjoy, and whether they play an instrument. Musical expertise can serve as a unifying factor, connecting different departments through a shared interest, fostering a sense of unity that extends beyond work and can be applied to customer interactions. These orientations were a great opportunity to share some of the same principles I'm sharing more in depth here in this book. The main goal was to show new employees that I hoped to be more than a group of people working together, but something more like a family. There's always a spark added to your life by knowing more people, getting more involved, and learning from others' unique perspective.

In thinking about this principle, I narrowed down to five the essential strengths that come from building a community of allies:

Enhanced creativity and innovation. This is the superpower, as far as I am concerned, in building a community of allies. Building a team of allies does not mean everyone thinks the same. Allies often have a common goal but different skills and interests. When people from diverse backgrounds and skill sets come together to collaborate, they bring unique perspectives and ideas to the table. This diversity of thought and experience can lead to opportunities and to more creative and innovative solutions to challenges. I see this every day in my work.

Increased efficiency and productivity. When you operate as a community of allies, it enables teams to work together toward a common goal, dividing tasks based on individual strengths and expertise. This distribution of labor can lead to increased efficiency and higher productivity as each team member can focus on what they do best. But the human factor must come first. Remember that productivity should be in the service of human needs.

Knowledge sharing and learning. In a collaborative environment, knowledge and expertise are freely exchanged among team members. This knowledge-sharing culture facilitates continuous learning and personal growth, benefiting both individuals and the organization as a whole.

Better decision-making. This is a point that cannot be made too often. Collaboration allows for multiple viewpoints to be considered when making critical decisions. My own experience is significant, but I cannot see all issues from every possible angle. Diversity of perspectives can lead to more informed and well-rounded choices, minimizing potential blind spots or biases. This is one of the major strengths of building a community of allies.

Improved communication. In a collaborative environment with as many partners and moving parts as we have at MIH, clear lines of communication are essential. We have protocols in place so our partners and working groups can communicate effectively within and beyond individual teams. Many companies found that the global pandemic forced them to become more strategic and intentional about pathways of communication. As MIH has grown over the past several years, we have taken lessons learned from our team and members of working groups to make sure clear communication happens at every level.

JOE CHENG ON MEETING JACK
AND BUILDING A COMMUNITY OF ALLIES

I got a message from Foxconn Chairman Young Liu's office. They were looking for talent to work on something new and very different. At first, I didn't see what a company known for manufacturing specific products would want with someone with my background. I didn't realize it at the time, but my experience and skills were a good match for a revolutionary open EV platform. I had come from a tech start-up background, and was working at Mozilla, exactly the kind of open and collaborative ecosystem Chairman Young was trying to build at MIH.

When they described the concept to me, I quickly became very interested. Community members from around the world? Yes. That makes sense. So, this open building and collaborating with community to build a product, this kind of experience, I thought, would be beneficial to MIH at that time as well.

My first meeting with Jack was a video remote meeting. Right away I could definitely feel that he has a lot of energy, and he embraces diversity. He wants to hear a lot of different opinions and perspectives. This stood out to me.

Jack is in a very unique position as a longtime insider to the automotive industry who is not shy about breaking down the traditional silos throughout the building process and supply chain. MIH is all about smashing those silos and collaborating to do great things.

Yet, without an insider at the helm, building a brand-new kind of automotive company would be incredibly difficult. Trying to enter the mode automotive industry is pretty difficult. But Jack knows everyone!

As we got off the ground at MIH, any supplier, partner, vendor, whoever we needed to reach out to, Jack was on his phone sending a message to the person. Between Ford, Fiat, and NIO, his personal community of allies is huge. It has been a major factor in building the open platform community of allies at MIH.

MIH, the company I currently head, is built on this principle. As an open platform for EV, we are developing new partnerships every day.

One such partner is VicOne, a major provider of cybersecurity software and services for the automotive industry. With MIH, VicOne is collaborating on an automotive cybersecurity white paper that will serve as a principal guideline for system developers and original equipment manufacturers when developing cybersecurity design.

CEO Max Cheng is our partner at VicOne, and he said this recently:

Emerging as an independent entity from Trend Micro with substantial revenue, our company has also actively participated in various open communities on the international stage. However, the automotive industry has traditionally been a closed ecosystem. Nonetheless, even before the establishment of MIH, Trend Micro had initiated independent projects targeting different automotive sectors. This presents a great opportunity as openness enables a better and more connected world.

In the future of mobility, security holds significant importance, particularly in the realm of software-defined vehicles. Recently, our industry has emphasized that safety alone is no longer sufficient; safety must be coupled with security. This is precisely what we recognize and value. Observing the success of open platforms in the automotive industry, we acknowledge their relative advantage. Trend Micro, being an internationally recognized company, has engaged in numerous lucrative endeavors. Originating from Taiwan, we are proud contributors to this positive trend. Furthermore, we continue to maintain a significant presence within MIH. Open platforms contribute immensely to security. Whenever an open platform emerges, we believe in collective participation and support.

While our primary objective is not profit-driven, I, on behalf of VicOne, firmly believe that these shared resources can benefit everyone, which is what I have been trying to persuade other partners at MIH.

An open platform provides active members with ample opportunities for interaction, facilitating the acquisition of domain knowledge from various fields. Increased collaboration among different industries generates additional commercial value.

Going It Alone Is Not An Option

We live in a world where it seems everyone is just looking out for number one. People who operate out of this frame of reference believe everything is transactional. When you operate this way, you have to stay alert because everyone is your enemy.

Of course, competitive advantage is important in business. But if you trust no one, you miss out on opportunities to collaborate and create profit for everyone.

I have seen this again and again in my career. Businesses that lack a collaborative spirit mostly do not last. There are always exceptions to the rule. But I have found in my interactions with colleagues from every sector of the automotive industry, companies that are too closed miss out on opportunities, and the culture within the company quickly becomes toxic, with everyone taking that "every person for themselves" mentality to their interactions within the company.

I can't live that way, and I've learned that a thriving business can't operate that way either.

Another example that comes to mind is from the cloud service, development platform, and tools working group at MIH.

We invited the nongovernmental organization Institute for Information Industry (III) to join the working group. They are in a collaborative effort to develop intelligent driving software and artificial intelligence and vehicle-to-vehicle communication technology as intelligent driving systems become a part of everyday life. This collaboration combines the power of software and hardware to keep this process moving forward. With the potency of cross-industry cooperation, they aim to create a more outstanding ecosystem for intelligent vehicles.

The collaboration between MIH and III includes the incorporation of internal wheel difference and safety warnings, making electric vehicle travel safer and providing greater peace of mind for road users. Through cloud-based data sharing in the future, the development of intelligent and convenient transportation services will create a smarter, safer, and greener sustainable transportation environment, bringing continuous progress and prosperity to society.

In Asian cultures, building a community of allies in this way, working together toward a common goal, is a fairly natural occurrence. At any rate, it is the only way I know how to do business, and it has served me well over the years. I believe surviving and thriving in the future will depend on our ability to adapt, find common cause, and work together.

Just one more example of this principle in action at MIH: we are part of a collaboration on vehicle-to-grid (V2G). This is a technology that enables energy to be pushed back to the power grid from the battery of an electric vehicle. This cooperation among Microsoft, Taipower, Yes Energy, and NextDrive creates end-to-end V2G solutions needed to work with energy suppliers, EV companies, energy storage systems, and chargers to form a complete electricity exchange and trading system.

However, with lack of a standard application programming interface (API) to allow different software programs to communicate with each other, this goal had been, up to this point, difficult to achieve. Before this, only vehicles and chargers had been capable of providing this return to the power grid. MIH convened a task force team to develop an API among these participants to exchange and share data to build a *first* end-to-end V2G demo in Taiwan.

How Do I Find My People?

In an earlier chapter, I shared some thoughts from my friend Bill Russo. Bill has been an auto executive in China for nearly twenty years. Bill currently works with Automobility as CEO.

A number of years ago, I invited Bill into the informal group playfully known as the Shanghai Mafia. We're just a group of people from different backgrounds who work in this industry. The only way we resemble any real mafia is that we consider each other family and do what we can to support and take care of each other.

Bill and I spoke recently about those early days. He remembers how he came to Shanghai and didn't know anybody. I invited him to join this motley crew of executives from all over the world. We became dear friends.

We talked about how this group of friends have scattered now. I and several others no longer live in Shanghai. If we are traveling and need a place to stay, Bill knows he has a place with me, as I know I do when I am traveling back there.

He reminded me of a time when he had invited me to speak at a conference he was putting together. He had given me the details, but I had a commitment to speak elsewhere on the same day. However, I arranged to videoconference into his conference at the right time. I was glad to do it, because I knew Bill would absolutely do the same thing for me.

As we wrapped up our recent conversation, Bill said:

"If you are part of the group, you get the help you need, no questions asked. You have your people who are gonna help you. We're all here to see a better tomorrow and to create a future that's as bright as we can make it. And getting there with people helping you move through that journey is much easier than if you've gotta fight the battle on your own."

I watch a History Channel show sometimes where people are dropped with only a handful of items into the deep forests of Canada or Alaska. The show is literally called *Alone*. It's the opposite of the CBS show *Survivor*, because everyone is totally isolated and expected to build shelter and hunt for food and live as long as they can by themselves.

Hardcore survivalists sometimes crumble in a matter of days under these isolated circumstances. The need for human contact and connection is too great. We cannot live well for very long without a community of allies. It is how we are hardwired. Thankfully, I don't have to live alone in the middle of a dense forest. I know who my people are, and I would never get by without them.

The MIH Consortium made a splash at CES, showcasing its electric vehicle innovations to international audiences.

PRINCIPLE 8

Adopt A Philosophy Of Harmony

Always aim at complete harmony of thought and word and deed.
— **MAHATMA GANDHI,** *Indian civil rights leader*

Music really is a way to reach out and hold on to each other in a healthy way.
— **STEVIE RAY VAUGHAN,** *American guitarist*

Harmony is right in the name of the company I lead: Mobility in *Harmony*. Harmony is incredibly important. This is a principle that many will recognize as a bedrock of Confucian thought. It is about creating the best results for the whole, not just basing life on individual satisfaction.

You can see how an open-source platform for creating EV products in a cohesive and workable supply chain fits into this philosophy. In work and all of life, a philosophy of harmony is necessary.

Elements That Shape A Philosophy Of Harmony

Harmony and balance are important in my culture, in Buddhism especially. Keeping everything in life in balance and harmony is important.

Following are just a few ways I try to foster harmony in my life and in the culture at MIH. You will see that a philosophy of harmony brings together and synthesizes many of the other principles I've explored throughout this book.

Balance interests. One of the most exciting aspects of MIH is how so many can work together from a shared platform. Balance is achieved because the potential of EV when it comes to the function of smart cities is so incredibly vast. And even though we are working toward similar goals, interests must remain in balance in order for these interconnected efforts to succeed.

As a business leader, balancing the interests of various stakeholders, such as employees, customers, suppliers, and shareholders, has never been more important. Harmony in business means striving to meet the needs of all parties involved, creating an environment where everyone feels respected and valued.

Engage in collaborative decision-making. I hope it has become very apparent that I value listening and learning that culminates in a collaborative approach to decision-making. I like to foster a culture in which all team members are invited to contribute their ideas and perspectives. Inclusion fosters a sense of belonging and mutual understanding, leading to better decisions and solutions.

Create win-win solutions. Harmony in business involves seeking win-win solutions rather than a zero-sum mentality.

Nurture relationships. Building and maintaining strong relationships is crucial to fostering harmony in business.

Employ emotional intelligence. Emotional intelligence should be valued, as it helps in understanding and managing emotions within the workplace. In whatever you do, operate with empathy, effective communication, and conflict resolution skills to handle challenging situations with sensitivity.

Adapt to change. If I couldn't adapt to change, I would still be selling cars run on fossil fuels through combustion engines. Embracing change while maintaining balance is an essential aspect of the philosophy of harmony.

Incorporate mindfulness and balance. Mindfulness practices can be used to cultivate a sense of balance in one's personal and professional lives. This could include practices like meditation or mindfulness exercises to reduce stress and improve decision-making.

You can see how all of these elements connect with the previous principles and build up to this experience of harmony.

Finding Harmony In Your Work

Ideals and principles are meant to be a guide in life. Does that mean I live a life of perfect harmony and balance at all times? Far from it. In the culture I grew up in, steeped in Buddhism, suffering is something recognized as very real. How do you find harmony when life happens, and you are faced with a challenge?

The 1980s were a fairly tumultuous time for the automobile industry. Detroit had been the world leader for so long, but it had been given a comeuppance by Japanese manufacturers who were building smaller cars with undeniably higher quality.

Ford learned these lessons quickly and I was really in the middle of all of that, dividing my time between China and the US, bridging some cultural divides, and bringing a lot of knowledge back and forth. Ford definitely came out of that time period stronger. This was the era of Ford: Quality is Job 1.

Today we face new challenges as the era of fossil fuels wanes. EV is the present and future of cars, but that doesn't mean the manufacturing, the infrastructure, and all of it comes easily or quickly.

To build harmony, we can find ways of working together. For instance, MIH collaborated on a powertrain project with American Axle & Manufacturing, Foxconn's Business Group C, Industrial Technology Research Institute, and Great Taiwan Gear. We built together a unique modular design of a three-in-one powertrain system, making MIH vehicle design more flexible and cost effective.

Harmony is a very important concept in Eastern culture. Think of the yin and yang symbol, where white and black are balanced. There is joy and there is sadness. When you work out, you expend energy, your body gets pushed to its limits. But you also feel that endorphin rush and you receive the health benefit from that workout after you push through the discomfort. You strive to complete a task, and you receive the results of your efforts. You work and you reap the rewards of that labor. A life in balance is not a life of shortcuts.

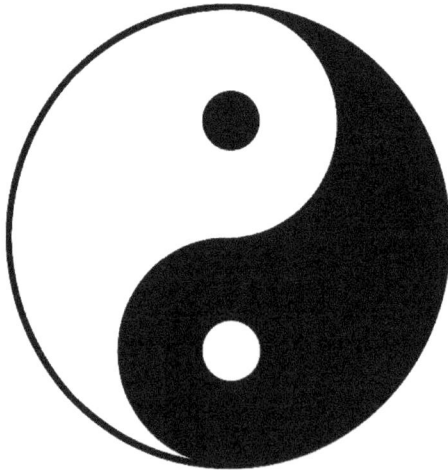

This symbol represents yin and yang, a complex relational concept in Chinese culture that has developed over thousands of years. Briefly put, the meaning of yin and yang is that the universe is governed by two opposing and complementing principles that can be observed in nature.

For me, a philosophy of harmony is about recognizing when I'm in a challenging situation and finding a path through that challenge: not ignoring difficulty but rather rising beyond it and learning from it.

Never Travel Without Your Guitar

Ken Hsi is head of sales and marketing at the Hsin Chong Ming Fong Group. I am friends with Ken's parents, and so I've known him since he was a little kid. Now he's a major part of HCMF. Time flies.

Part of a philosophy of harmony is showing up for people and exemplifying, as best you can, the principles you live by. For me, living a life of harmony means that music is never far away. As often as possible, it's as close as my guitar case.

I appreciate this memory Ken recently shared with me:

I still remember it was not long after I took over HCMF's sales and marketing department. It was on a hot summer day; I was flying back from Changsha after a business meeting with our local joint venture plant partner. As I was sitting in my seat on a China Airlines flight, reading a book, aboard came a guy with a large carry-on guitar case, sitting right next to me. At the time I didn't realize it was Jack, since I was focused on my own doing. Then a familiar voiced called out to me "Hao-hao, long time no see." Hao-hao is my Chinese name and Jack has been calling me by that nickname since I can remember.

I was surprised, but at the same time not so surprised to see him, because I knew at the time he was the head of the Fiat group for the greater China region, which is based out of Changsha, so I kind of knew one day or the other I would run into him eventually. I put down my book and we started to chat, for the entire four hours we just kept on chatting. That was actually the first time I chatted with Jack alone this long, since I started my working career. I was a newbie to the business at the time, I had so many questions I would like to ask for his advice. I can remember clearly, he started out by saying, "Hey, I don't want this to be a lecture, but a moment of sharing." Then he started to talk about his guitar and told me he would not go anywhere without it. We talked about his music dreams and how he incorporates it into his life and uses it to affect everyone around him. He said when he or the people around him feel down, he will just pick up the guitar and sing a song for them, to cheer them up. He even invites them to join from time to time. He said, "There is no life without a happy life." And music is the way he uses to pass on that message to others.

Jack loves his work as much as he loves his life. He treats every experience as a challenge and tries to make the best out of it. He told me that if we don't like what we do, we can never do the work well. So, we need to learn to love our work, just as much as we love our lives. Be motivated all the time, be eager for new knowledge, and be as receptive to the outside environment as much as possible; that is the way to progress in work and in life. He is the most energized and accepting person I have ever met.

Then we talked about work, and I asked a million questions about how to advance with my work and how his experiences can help me understand more about my work. He held nothing back and answered every question that I asked—that is just who he is, a helpful and sharing person. He told me never to stop learning and always look ahead instead of looking back; give everything and more to the things that you are doing, make sure there are no regrets. That talk on the flight still helps me whenever I need insight at work today.

His words often come back to my mind when I am in trouble or in need. To me, he is more than just a business partner or family friend. He is someone I look up to and see as a mentor.

HCMF has been a part of MIH from the very beginning. They are part of several working groups, and an integral member of the team working on Project X, the smart mobility initiative.

Jack, with guitar in hand, lives his musical dream and inspires others to pursue passions beyond work.

Realism, Not Just Idealism

The pursuit of harmony in life is not merely an idealistic notion; it is a fundamental necessity for our well-being and fulfillment. Harmony encompasses the delicate balance among various facets of our existence, from our relationships with others to our relationship with ourselves, and even our connection to the natural world. To put it in musical terms, it is how we weave together life's bittersweet symphony.

In a world often marked by chaos and discord, the pursuit of harmony is a noble and worthwhile endeavor. It is the only path forward that I know.

Jack Cheng at the CNBC panel 'Managing Asia: Getting Asia Future Ready' in Bangkok, joining esteemed leaders to discuss the continent's path forward

EPILOGUE

Your Next Chapter

I believe very strongly that corporations could and should be a major force for resolving social and environmental concerns in the twenty-first century.

—**WILLIAM CLAY FORD JR.**, *executive chair of Ford Motor Company*

The biggest emotion in creation is the bridge to optimism.

—**BRIAN MAY**, *British astrophysicist, lead guitarist for the band Queen*

Harmony is not just a musical term; it is a way of life. Writing or thinking about principles is easy. Living by them takes discipline. I have tried over my life to build these principles into habits that stand the test of time. They see me through no matter where the path of life takes me.

Principles are there as guides. You will make mistakes along the way, but hopefully you see these mistakes for the learning opportunities they are.

Did I imagine exactly this path for myself back when I started with Ford? Absolutely not. I was looking for a job and a chance to enjoy some of the best music in the world. People have started with a lot less!

That Bill Ford quote above means a lot to me. These concerns were not on my mind when I started in this industry, but I am sure they are at least in the back of your mind as a young leader. It is impossible to see the road too far ahead of us, but I have learned to trust in myself and the principles that guide me to get me safely past the next road marker.

Signposts On The Road To What's Next

At the risk of sounding like a commencement speaker, I want to leave you with a few key strategies for using these eight principles to navigate the next stages of your life and career:

Set clear goals. You know that (lazy) interview question, "Where do you see yourself in five years?" That's actually an important question to keep asking yourself outside the job search. What do you want to achieve in the next stage of your career? Having a clear sense of direction, written down somewhere and reviewed and revised often, will guide your decisions and actions.

Continuously learn. Invest in your professional development. Keep reading books like this, and take advantage of learning opportunities offered by your company. Stay updated on industry trends, take pertinent courses, attend workshops, and consider pursuing advanced degrees or certifications.

Network. Build and maintain a strong professional network. If you are more introverted, find ways of connecting with people using online tools as well as meeting new people in person. Push yourself. Attend industry events, join relevant associations, and connect with mentors who can provide guidance and support.

Keep honing leadership skills. As your career develops, more responsibility will be required of you. Find mentors who can help you develop leadership skills based on your personal style. Not everyone leads with a guitar in one hand, but it has always worked for me!

Build a personal brand. This is an area where I learn so much from my younger team members. It is a TikTok world out there, and you need to know how to establish a strong personal brand that reflects your values, skills, and expertise. This can set you apart in a competitive job market.

Seek feedback. Find people who will give it to you straight without tearing you down. Constructive feedback can help you identify areas for improvement.

Think strategically. Strategic thinking is a too-often overlooked skill. Develop your ability to think strategically. Understand your organization's goals and how your role contributes to achieving them. Find ways to enhance your role to better meet your organization's objectives.

Develop financial literacy. Living in the United States, I was surprised at how financial literacy was not a part of everyday learning for students. As you advance, financial acumen becomes increasingly important, so you understand your company's finances as well as your personal finances.

Manage time effectively. Time is not a renewable resource. Effective time management is crucial. Prioritize tasks, delegate when necessary, and focus on high-impact activities.

Be resilient. Not everything will go according to plan. The journey to the next stage of your career may have setbacks. Stay resilient, persevere through challenges, and maintain a positive attitude.

Stay inquisitive. Your questions are like currency. They have value, especially as you seek answers that spawn new questions. Cultivate curiosity. Ask questions, seek to understand, and never stop learning.

Build a diverse skill set. The things you do and the way you do them will change over time. When I started work at Ford, we used typewriters and fax machines. People who are stuck in their ways and refuse to learn new skills are quickly replaced. Diversify your abilities and knowledge to be more adaptable and valuable to your organization.

Plan for the long term. Think about your career in the long term. What legacy do you want to leave? What impact do you want to make?

Stay humble. Regardless of your success, remain humble and approachable. Treat everyone with respect and empathy.

Life comes at you fast, and it's okay to take your time and learn along the way. Keep these principles in mind, and you'll be better equipped to navigate the next stage of your career successfully.

What does the next stage hold for me? MIH has many projects in the pipeline through our various working groups. It is an exciting time to be in this industry, a time when technology is breaking down barriers to collaboration and cooperation among companies that might otherwise be keeping their distance in order to protect intellectual property. An open and agnostic system means we can work together to solve bigger problems than we could as separate entities hiding away in our own R and D labs.

I am excited at where my career has taken me, here leading MIH. When Chairman Young Liu invited me to take on the role of CEO, I jumped at the chance. I could be riding off into the sunset like a weathered cowboy in an old Hollywood Western. But I have more to learn and more to share.

Jack introduced the open and agnostic concept of Project X to attendees at CES 2023.

Amid a highly successful press event by MIH at Japan, numerous journalists engage in interviewing Jack, capturing the momentum and excitement of the occasion.

ACKNOWLEDGMENTS

The American writer Ralph Waldo Emerson once said, "Nothing great was ever achieved without enthusiasm." I agree and would like to add nothing great was ever achieved without the enthusiastic support of others.

There are many to thank for their enthusiastic support, starting with Mr. Young Liu, the chairman of Hon Hai Technology Group (Foxconn), and the entire Foxconn team.

Let me also express gratitude to the MIH Consortium Board of Directors: David Huang, James Tu, and Steven Yu. In addition, thanks to the entire MIH team for their dedication to our mission.

This book is about the special relationships I have been blessed with through the years. A special debt of gratitude to all partners and friends featured or interviewed in the book.

An author is only as good as the editorial team they partner with, and I want to thank Leslie Rubin, Henry DeVries, Craig Landes, and Devin DeVries for making this dream project of mine a reality.

Finally, a special thank you and love to my family and friends from around the globe who have connected wholeheartedly and contributed to this special journey. I could not have done it without you.

ABOUT THE AUTHOR

Jack Cheng, an auto industry veteran with forty years of experience in the industry, was named CEO of the Foxconn-backed MIH Consortium in 2021. He drives the development of the software and hardware platform for electric vehicles (EV).

Cheng is one of the co-founders of the EV company NIO, and his tenure there saw his significant contributions to the firm's supply chain, industrialization, and driving technology.

Prior to joining MIH Consortium, Cheng was the Managing Director of Fiat China, Chairman of XPT, and he held senior leadership positions in Magneti Marelli Asia-Pacific and Ford Motor Company.

WORKS CITED
AND AUTHOR'S NOTES

1   Scott Miller, "Don't Know Your Professional Values? You Might Be on the Wrong Track," *Inc.*, April 23, 2021, https://www.inc.com/scott-miller/dont-know-your-professional-values-you-might-be-on-wrong-track.html.

2   John Knotts, "Seven Ways to Become a Human-Centered Business," *Forbes*, June 12, 2023, https://www.forbes.com/sites/forbescoachescouncil/2023/06/12/seven-ways-to-become-a-human-centered-business/?sh=28fc5ab85e74.

3   Ted Lien, "Testing and certification are the cornerstones of EV; MIH never compromises on safety!" MIH Insights, November 28, 2022. https://www.mih-ev.org/en/market/2034

4   More details can be found here: https://www.mih-ev.org/en/news/740 and https://www.energytrend.com/news/20220113-25707.html.

5   Tomas Chamorro-Premuzic, "How to Love Your Job According to Science," *Fast Company*, February 28, 2022, https://www.fastcompany.com/90725498/how-to-love-your-job-according-to-science.

6   Peter Singer, *The Most Good You Can Do* (New Haven, CT: Yale University Press, 2015).

7   Palena Neal, "'Serious' Leaders Need Self-Care, Too," *Harvard Business Review*, October 22, 2020, https://hbr. org/2020/10/serious-leaders-need-self-care-too.

8   Chris Hunter, "This Science-Backed Growth Mindset Strategy Can Boost Your Success in Work and Life," *Fast Company*, May 15, 2021, https://www.fastcompany. com/90635257/this-science-backed-growth-mindset-strategy-can-boost-your-success-in-work-and-life.

9   Daniel H. Pink, *Drive: The Surprising Truth About What Motivates Us* (New York: Riverhead Books, 2009.)

10 James Clear, *Atomic Habits: An Easy & Proven Way to Build Good Habits & Break Bad Ones* (New York: Avery, 2018)

11 Simon Sinek, *Start with Why: How Great Leaders Inspire Everyone to Take Action*, (New York: Portfolio, 2011).

12 David Byrne, vocalist, "Once in a Lifetime," by David Byrne, Brian Eno, Chris Frantz, Jerry Harrison, and Tina Weymouth, track 1 on side 2 on *Remain in Light*, Sire R1 70802, 1980, 33 1/3 rpm.

13 Ringo Starr, vocalist, "With a Little Help from My Friends," by John Lennon and Paul McCartney, track 2 on side 1 on *Sgt. Pepper's Lonely Hearts Club Band*, Parlophone PCS 7027, 1967, 33 1/3 rpm.

INDEX